Debt Payment Tracker

Belongs To:

_____

Debt Payment Tracker

Creditor		Target Payoff Date	
Account No.		Credit Type	

Starting Balance		Min. Payment	
Credit Limit		Interest Rate	

Date	Amount	Balance	Notes
Total			

Debt Payment Tracker

Creditor	Target Payoff Date
Account No.	Credit Type

Starting Balance	Min. Payment
Credit Limit	Interest Rate

Date	Amount	Balance	Notes
Total			

Debt Payment Tracker

Creditor		Target Payoff Date	
Account No.		Credit Type	

Starting Balance		Min. Payment	
Credit Limit		Interest Rate	

Date	Amount	Balance	Notes
Total			

Debt Payment Tracker

Creditor		Target Payoff Date	
Account No.		Credit Type	

Starting Balance		Min. Payment	
Credit Limit		Interest Rate	

Date	Amount	Balance	Notes
Total			

Debt Payment Tracker

Creditor		Target Payoff Date	
Account No.		Credit Type	

Starting Balance		Min. Payment	
Credit Limit		Interest Rate	

Date	Amount	Balance	Notes
Total			

Debt Payment Tracker

Creditor		Target Payoff Date	
Account No.		Credit Type	

Starting Balance		Min. Payment	
Credit Limit		Interest Rate	

Date	Amount	Balance	Notes
Total			

Debt Payment Tracker

Creditor		Target Payoff Date	
Account No.		Credit Type	

Starting Balance		Min. Payment	
Credit Limit		Interest Rate	

Date	Amount	Balance	Notes
Total			

Debt Payment Tracker

Creditor	
Account No.	

Target Payoff Date	
Credit Type	

Starting Balance	
Credit Limit	

Min. Payment	
Interest Rate	

Date	Amount	Balance	Notes
Total			

Debt Payment Tracker

Creditor		Target Payoff Date	
Account No.		Credit Type	
Starting Balance		Min. Payment	
Credit Limit		Interest Rate	

Date	Amount	Balance	Notes
Total			

Debt Payment Tracker

Creditor		Target Payoff Date	
Account No.		Credit Type	
Starting Balance		Min. Payment	
Credit Limit		Interest Rate	

Date	Amount	Balance	Notes
Total			

Debt Payment Tracker

Creditor		Target Payoff Date	
Account No.		Credit Type	

Starting Balance		Min. Payment	
Credit Limit		Interest Rate	

Date	Amount	Balance	Notes
Total			

Debt Payment Tracker

Creditor	Target Payoff Date
Account No.	Credit Type

Starting Balance	Min. Payment
Credit Limit	Interest Rate

Date	Amount	Balance	Notes
Total			

Debt Payment Tracker

Creditor	
Account No.	

Target Payoff Date	
Credit Type	

Starting Balance	
Credit Limit	

Min. Payment	
Interest Rate	

Date	Amount	Balance	Notes
Total			

Debt Payment Tracker

Creditor		Target Payoff Date	
Account No.		Credit Type	
Starting Balance		Min. Payment	
Credit Limit		Interest Rate	

Date	Amount	Balance	Notes
Total			

Debt Payment Tracker

Creditor		Target Payoff Date	
Account No.		Credit Type	

Starting Balance		Min. Payment	
Credit Limit		Interest Rate	

Date	Amount	Balance	Notes
Total			

Debt Payment Tracker

Creditor		Target Payoff Date	
Account No.		Credit Type	

Starting Balance		Min. Payment	
Credit Limit		Interest Rate	

Date	Amount	Balance	Notes
Total			

Debt Payment Tracker

| Creditor | | Target Payoff Date |
| Account No. | | Credit Type |

| Starting Balance | | Min. Payment |
| Credit Limit | | Interest Rate |

Date	Amount	Balance	Notes
Total			

Debt Payment Tracker

Creditor		Target Payoff Date	
Account No.		Credit Type	

Starting Balance		Min. Payment	
Credit Limit		Interest Rate	

Date	Amount	Balance	Notes
Total			

Debt Payment Tracker

Creditor		Target Payoff Date	
Account No.		Credit Type	

Starting Balance		Min. Payment	
Credit Limit		Interest Rate	

Date	Amount	Balance	Notes
Total			

Debt Payment Tracker

Creditor		Target Payoff Date	
Account No.		Credit Type	

Starting Balance		Min. Payment	
Credit Limit		Interest Rate	

Date	Amount	Balance	Notes
Total			

Debt Payment Tracker

Creditor		Target Payoff Date	
Account No.		Credit Type	

Starting Balance		Min. Payment	
Credit Limit		Interest Rate	

Date	Amount	Balance	Notes
Total			

Debt Payment Tracker

Creditor		Target Payoff Date	
Account No.		Credit Type	

Starting Balance		Min. Payment	
Credit Limit		Interest Rate	

Date	Amount	Balance	Notes
Total			

Debt Payment Tracker

Creditor		Target Payoff Date	
Account No.		Credit Type	

Starting Balance		Min. Payment	
Credit Limit		Interest Rate	

Date	Amount	Balance	Notes
Total			

Debt Payment Tracker

Creditor	
Account No.	

Target Payoff Date	
Credit Type	

Starting Balance	
Credit Limit	

Min. Payment	
Interest Rate	

Date	Amount	Balance	Notes
Total			

Debt Payment Tracker

Creditor		Target Payoff Date	
Account No.		Credit Type	

Starting Balance		Min. Payment	
Credit Limit		Interest Rate	

Date	Amount	Balance	Notes
Total			

Debt Payment Tracker

Creditor		Target Payoff Date	
Account No.		Credit Type	

Starting Balance		Min. Payment	
Credit Limit		Interest Rate	

Date	Amount	Balance	Notes
Total			

Debt Payment Tracker

- Creditor
- Account No.

- Target Payoff Date
- Credit Type

- Starting Balance
- Credit Limit

- Min. Payment
- Interest Rate

Date	Amount	Balance	Notes
Total			

Debt Payment Tracker

Creditor
Account No.

Target Payoff Date
Credit Type

Starting Balance
Credit Limit

Min. Payment
Interest Rate

Date	Amount	Balance	Notes
Total			

Debt Payment Tracker

Creditor		Target Payoff Date	
Account No.		Credit Type	

Starting Balance		Min. Payment	
Credit Limit		Interest Rate	

Date	Amount	Balance	Notes
Total			

Debt Payment Tracker

Creditor		Target Payoff Date	
Account No.		Credit Type	
Starting Balance		Min. Payment	
Credit Limit		Interest Rate	

Date	Amount	Balance	Notes
Total			

Debt Payment Tracker

Creditor		Target Payoff Date	
Account No.		Credit Type	

Starting Balance		Min. Payment	
Credit Limit		Interest Rate	

Date	Amount	Balance	Notes
Total			

Debt Payment Tracker

Creditor		Target Payoff Date	
Account No.		Credit Type	
Starting Balance		Min. Payment	
Credit Limit		Interest Rate	

Date	Amount	Balance	Notes
Total			

Debt Payment Tracker

Creditor		Target Payoff Date	
Account No.		Credit Type	

Starting Balance		Min. Payment	
Credit Limit		Interest Rate	

Date	Amount	Balance	Notes
Total			

Debt Payment Tracker

Creditor		Target Payoff Date	
Account No.		Credit Type	

Starting Balance		Min. Payment	
Credit Limit		Interest Rate	

Date	Amount	Balance	Notes
Total			

Debt Payment Tracker

Creditor	Target Payoff Date
Account No.	Credit Type

Starting Balance	Min. Payment
Credit Limit	Interest Rate

Date	Amount	Balance	Notes
Total			

Debt Payment Tracker

Creditor		Target Payoff Date	
Account No.		Credit Type	
Starting Balance		Min. Payment	
Credit Limit		Interest Rate	

Date	Amount	Balance	Notes
Total			

Debt Payment Tracker

Creditor		Target Payoff Date	
Account No.		Credit Type	

Starting Balance		Min. Payment	
Credit Limit		Interest Rate	

Date	Amount	Balance	Notes
Total			

Debt Payment Tracker

Creditor:
Account No.:

Target Payoff Date:
Credit Type:

Starting Balance:
Credit Limit:

Min. Payment:
Interest Rate:

Date	Amount	Balance	Notes
Total			

Debt Payment Tracker

Creditor		Target Payoff Date	
Account No.		Credit Type	
Starting Balance		Min. Payment	
Credit Limit		Interest Rate	

Date	Amount	Balance	Notes
Total			

Debt Payment Tracker

Creditor		Target Payoff Date	
Account No.		Credit Type	
Starting Balance		Min. Payment	
Credit Limit		Interest Rate	

Date	Amount	Balance	Notes
Total			

Debt Payment Tracker

Creditor		Target Payoff Date	
Account No.		Credit Type	

Starting Balance		Min. Payment	
Credit Limit		Interest Rate	

Date	Amount	Balance	Notes
Total			

Debt Payment Tracker

Creditor

Account No.

Starting Balance

Credit Limit

Target Payoff Date

Credit Type

Min. Payment

Interest Rate

Date	Amount	Balance	Notes
Total			

Debt Payment Tracker

Creditor		Target Payoff Date	
Account No.		Credit Type	

Starting Balance		Min. Payment	
Credit Limit		Interest Rate	

Date	Amount	Balance	Notes
Total			

Debt Payment Tracker

Creditor		Target Payoff Date	
Account No.		Credit Type	

Starting Balance		Min. Payment	
Credit Limit		Interest Rate	

Date	Amount	Balance	Notes
Total			

Debt Payment Tracker

Creditor		Target Payoff Date	
Account No.		Credit Type	

Starting Balance		Min. Payment	
Credit Limit		Interest Rate	

Date	Amount	Balance	Notes
Total			

Debt Payment Tracker

Creditor	
Account No.	

Starting Balance	
Credit Limit	

Target Payoff Date	
Credit Type	

Min. Payment	
Interest Rate	

Date	Amount	Balance	Notes
Total			

Debt Payment Tracker

Creditor		Target Payoff Date	
Account No.		Credit Type	

Starting Balance		Min. Payment	
Credit Limit		Interest Rate	

Date	Amount	Balance	Notes
Total			

Debt Payment Tracker

Creditor		Target Payoff Date	
Account No.		Credit Type	
Starting Balance		Min. Payment	
Credit Limit		Interest Rate	

Date	Amount	Balance	Notes
Total			

Debt Payment Tracker

Creditor		Target Payoff Date	
Account No.		Credit Type	

Starting Balance		Min. Payment	
Credit Limit		Interest Rate	

Date	Amount	Balance	Notes
Total			

Debt Payment Tracker

Creditor		Target Payoff Date	
Account No.		Credit Type	
Starting Balance		Min. Payment	
Credit Limit		Interest Rate	

Date	Amount	Balance	Notes
Total			

Debt Payment Tracker

Creditor		Target Payoff Date	
Account No.		Credit Type	

Starting Balance		Min. Payment	
Credit Limit		Interest Rate	

Date	Amount	Balance	Notes
Total			

Debt Payment Tracker

Creditor
Account No.

Target Payoff Date
Credit Type

Starting Balance
Credit Limit

Min. Payment
Interest Rate

Date	Amount	Balance	Notes
Total			

Debt Payment Tracker

Creditor		Target Payoff Date	
Account No.		Credit Type	

Starting Balance		Min. Payment	
Credit Limit		Interest Rate	

Date	Amount	Balance	Notes
Total			

Debt Payment Tracker

Creditor		Target Payoff Date	
Account No.		Credit Type	

Starting Balance		Min. Payment	
Credit Limit		Interest Rate	

Date	Amount	Balance	Notes
Total			

Debt Payment Tracker

Creditor		Target Payoff Date	
Account No.		Credit Type	

Starting Balance		Min. Payment	
Credit Limit		Interest Rate	

Date	Amount	Balance	Notes
Total			

Debt Payment Tracker

Creditor		Target Payoff Date	
Account No.		Credit Type	

Starting Balance		Min. Payment	
Credit Limit		Interest Rate	

Date	Amount	Balance	Notes
Total			

Debt Payment Tracker

Creditor		Target Payoff Date	
Account No.		Credit Type	

Starting Balance		Min. Payment	
Credit Limit		Interest Rate	

Date	Amount	Balance	Notes
Total			

Debt Payment Tracker

Creditor		Target Payoff Date	
Account No.		Credit Type	
Starting Balance		Min. Payment	
Credit Limit		Interest Rate	

Date	Amount	Balance	Notes
Total			

Debt Payment Tracker

Creditor		Target Payoff Date	
Account No.		Credit Type	

Starting Balance		Min. Payment	
Credit Limit		Interest Rate	

Date	Amount	Balance	Notes
Total			

Debt Payment Tracker

Creditor	
Account No.	

Target Payoff Date	
Credit Type	

Starting Balance	
Credit Limit	

Min. Payment	
Interest Rate	

Date	Amount	Balance	Notes
Total			

Debt Payment Tracker

Creditor		Target Payoff Date	
Account No.		Credit Type	

Starting Balance		Min. Payment	
Credit Limit		Interest Rate	

Date	Amount	Balance	Notes
Total			

Debt Payment Tracker

Creditor		Target Payoff Date	
Account No.		Credit Type	

Starting Balance		Min. Payment	
Credit Limit		Interest Rate	

Date	Amount	Balance	Notes
Total			

Debt Payment Tracker

Creditor		Target Payoff Date	
Account No.		Credit Type	

Starting Balance		Min. Payment	
Credit Limit		Interest Rate	

Date	Amount	Balance	Notes
Total			

Debt Payment Tracker

Creditor		Target Payoff Date	
Account No.		Credit Type	

Starting Balance		Min. Payment	
Credit Limit		Interest Rate	

Date	Amount	Balance	Notes
Total			

Debt Payment Tracker

Creditor		Target Payoff Date	
Account No.		Credit Type	

Starting Balance		Min. Payment	
Credit Limit		Interest Rate	

Date	Amount	Balance	Notes
Total			

Debt Payment Tracker

Creditor		Target Payoff Date	
Account No.		Credit Type	

Starting Balance		Min. Payment	
Credit Limit		Interest Rate	

Date	Amount	Balance	Notes
Total			

Debt Payment Tracker

Creditor		Target Payoff Date	
Account No.		Credit Type	

Starting Balance		Min. Payment	
Credit Limit		Interest Rate	

Date	Amount	Balance	Notes
Total			

Debt Payment Tracker

Creditor		Target Payoff Date	
Account No.		Credit Type	

Starting Balance		Min. Payment	
Credit Limit		Interest Rate	

Date	Amount	Balance	Notes
Total			

Debt Payment Tracker

Creditor		Target Payoff Date	
Account No.		Credit Type	

Starting Balance		Min. Payment	
Credit Limit		Interest Rate	

Date	Amount	Balance	Notes
Total			

Debt Payment Tracker

Creditor:
Account No.:

Target Payoff Date:
Credit Type:

Starting Balance:
Credit Limit:

Min. Payment:
Interest Rate:

Date	Amount	Balance	Notes
Total			

Debt Payment Tracker

Creditor		Target Payoff Date	
Account No.		Credit Type	

Starting Balance		Min. Payment	
Credit Limit		Interest Rate	

Date	Amount	Balance	Notes
Total			

Debt Payment Tracker

Creditor		Target Payoff Date	
Account No.		Credit Type	

Starting Balance		Min. Payment	
Credit Limit		Interest Rate	

Date	Amount	Balance	Notes
Total			

Debt Payment Tracker

Creditor		Target Payoff Date	
Account No.		Credit Type	

Starting Balance		Min. Payment	
Credit Limit		Interest Rate	

Date	Amount	Balance	Notes
Total			

Debt Payment Tracker

Creditor		Target Payoff Date	
Account No.		Credit Type	
Starting Balance		Min. Payment	
Credit Limit		Interest Rate	

Date	Amount	Balance	Notes
Total			

Debt Payment Tracker

Creditor		Target Payoff Date	
Account No.		Credit Type	

Starting Balance		Min. Payment	
Credit Limit		Interest Rate	

Date	Amount	Balance	Notes
Total			

Debt Payment Tracker

Creditor		Target Payoff Date	
Account No.		Credit Type	
Starting Balance		Min. Payment	
Credit Limit		Interest Rate	

Date	Amount	Balance	Notes
Total			

Debt Payment Tracker

Creditor		Target Payoff Date	
Account No.		Credit Type	

Starting Balance		Min. Payment	
Credit Limit		Interest Rate	

Date	Amount	Balance	Notes
Total			

Debt Payment Tracker

Creditor		Target Payoff Date	
Account No.		Credit Type	
Starting Balance		Min. Payment	
Credit Limit		Interest Rate	

Date	Amount	Balance	Notes
Total			

Debt Payment Tracker

Creditor		Target Payoff Date	
Account No.		Credit Type	

Starting Balance		Min. Payment	
Credit Limit		Interest Rate	

Date	Amount	Balance	Notes
Total			

Debt Payment Tracker

Creditor		Target Payoff Date	
Account No.		Credit Type	
Starting Balance		Min. Payment	
Credit Limit		Interest Rate	

Date	Amount	Balance	Notes
Total			

Debt Payment Tracker

Creditor		Target Payoff Date
Account No.		Credit Type

Starting Balance		Min. Payment
Credit Limit		Interest Rate

Date	Amount	Balance	Notes
Total			

Debt Payment Tracker

Creditor		Target Payoff Date	
Account No.		Credit Type	
Starting Balance		Min. Payment	
Credit Limit		Interest Rate	

Date	Amount	Balance	Notes
Total			

Debt Payment Tracker

Creditor		Target Payoff Date	
Account No.		Credit Type	

Starting Balance		Min. Payment	
Credit Limit		Interest Rate	

Date	Amount	Balance	Notes
Total			

Debt Payment Tracker

Creditor		Target Payoff Date	
Account No.		Credit Type	
Starting Balance		Min. Payment	
Credit Limit		Interest Rate	

Date	Amount	Balance	Notes
Total			

Debt Payment Tracker

Creditor	
Account No.	

Target Payoff Date	
Credit Type	

Starting Balance	
Credit Limit	

Min. Payment	
Interest Rate	

Date	Amount	Balance	Notes
Total			

Debt Payment Tracker

Creditor		Target Payoff Date	
Account No.		Credit Type	
Starting Balance		Min. Payment	
Credit Limit		Interest Rate	

Date	Amount	Balance	Notes
Total			

Debt Payment Tracker

Creditor		Target Payoff Date	
Account No.		Credit Type	

Starting Balance		Min. Payment	
Credit Limit		Interest Rate	

Date	Amount	Balance	Notes
Total			

Debt Payment Tracker

Creditor		Target Payoff Date	
Account No.		Credit Type	

Starting Balance		Min. Payment	
Credit Limit		Interest Rate	

Date	Amount	Balance	Notes
Total			

Debt Payment Tracker

Creditor		Target Payoff Date	
Account No.		Credit Type	

Starting Balance		Min. Payment	
Credit Limit		Interest Rate	

Date	Amount	Balance	Notes
Total			

Debt Payment Tracker

Creditor		Target Payoff Date	
Account No.		Credit Type	
Starting Balance		Min. Payment	
Credit Limit		Interest Rate	

Date	Amount	Balance	Notes
Total			

Debt Payment Tracker

Creditor		Target Payoff Date	
Account No.		Credit Type	

Starting Balance		Min. Payment	
Credit Limit		Interest Rate	

Date	Amount	Balance	Notes
Total			

Debt Payment Tracker

Creditor		Target Payoff Date	
Account No.		Credit Type	
Starting Balance		Min. Payment	
Credit Limit		Interest Rate	

Date	Amount	Balance	Notes
Total			

Debt Payment Tracker

Creditor		Target Payoff Date	
Account No.		Credit Type	
Starting Balance		Min. Payment	
Credit Limit		Interest Rate	

Date	Amount	Balance	Notes
Total			

Debt Payment Tracker

Creditor		Target Payoff Date	
Account No.		Credit Type	
Starting Balance		Min. Payment	
Credit Limit		Interest Rate	

Date	Amount	Balance	Notes
Total			

Debt Payment Tracker

Creditor		Target Payoff Date	
Account No.		Credit Type	

Starting Balance		Min. Payment	
Credit Limit		Interest Rate	

Date	Amount	Balance	Notes
Total			

Debt Payment Tracker

Creditor		Target Payoff Date	
Account No.		Credit Type	
Starting Balance		Min. Payment	
Credit Limit		Interest Rate	

Date	Amount	Balance	Notes
Total			

Debt Payment Tracker

Creditor		Target Payoff Date	
Account No.		Credit Type	

Starting Balance		Min. Payment	
Credit Limit		Interest Rate	

Date	Amount	Balance	Notes
Total			

Debt Payment Tracker

Creditor		Target Payoff Date	
Account No.		Credit Type	
Starting Balance		Min. Payment	
Credit Limit		Interest Rate	

Date	Amount	Balance	Notes
Total			

Debt Payment Tracker

Creditor		Target Payoff Date	
Account No.		Credit Type	
Starting Balance		Min. Payment	
Credit Limit		Interest Rate	

Date	Amount	Balance	Notes
Total			

Debt Payment Tracker

Creditor		Target Payoff Date	
Account No.		Credit Type	

Starting Balance		Min. Payment	
Credit Limit		Interest Rate	

Date	Amount	Balance	Notes
Total			

Debt Payment Tracker

Creditor		Target Payoff Date	
Account No.		Credit Type	

Starting Balance		Min. Payment	
Credit Limit		Interest Rate	

Date	Amount	Balance	Notes
Total			

Debt Payment Tracker

Creditor		Target Payoff Date	
Account No.		Credit Type	

Starting Balance		Min. Payment	
Credit Limit		Interest Rate	

Date	Amount	Balance	Notes
Total			

Debt Payment Tracker

Creditor
Account No.

Target Payoff Date
Credit Type

Starting Balance
Credit Limit

Min. Payment
Interest Rate

Date	Amount	Balance	Notes
Total			

Debt Payment Tracker

Creditor		Target Payoff Date	
Account No.		Credit Type	

Starting Balance		Min. Payment	
Credit Limit		Interest Rate	

Date	Amount	Balance	Notes
Total			

Debt Payment Tracker

Creditor		Target Payoff Date	
Account No.		Credit Type	

Starting Balance		Min. Payment	
Credit Limit		Interest Rate	

Date	Amount	Balance	Notes
Total			

Debt Payment Tracker

Creditor	
Account No.	

Target Payoff Date	
Credit Type	

Starting Balance	
Credit Limit	

Min. Payment	
Interest Rate	

Date	Amount	Balance	Notes
Total			

Debt Payment Tracker

Creditor		Target Payoff Date	
Account No.		Credit Type	

Starting Balance		Min. Payment	
Credit Limit		Interest Rate	

Date	Amount	Balance	Notes
Total			

Debt Payment Tracker

Creditor		Target Payoff Date	
Account No.		Credit Type	
Starting Balance		Min. Payment	
Credit Limit		Interest Rate	

Date	Amount	Balance	Notes
Total			

www.ingramcontent.com/pod-product-compliance
Lightning Source LLC
Chambersburg PA
CBHW080550220526
45466CB00010B/3099